Technology and the Civil War

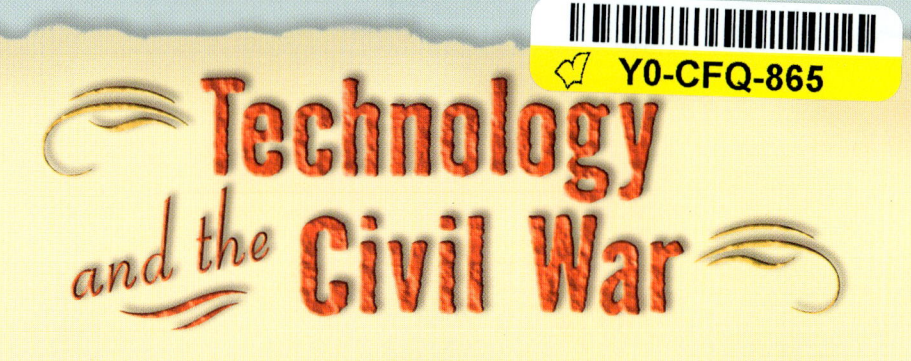

by A. J. Crozier

Table of Contents

Introduction 2

Chapter 1
The Tools of War 4

Chapter 2
Medical Care in the War 12

Chapter 3
The Spread of Information 22

Conclusion 30

Glossary 31

Index 32

Introduction

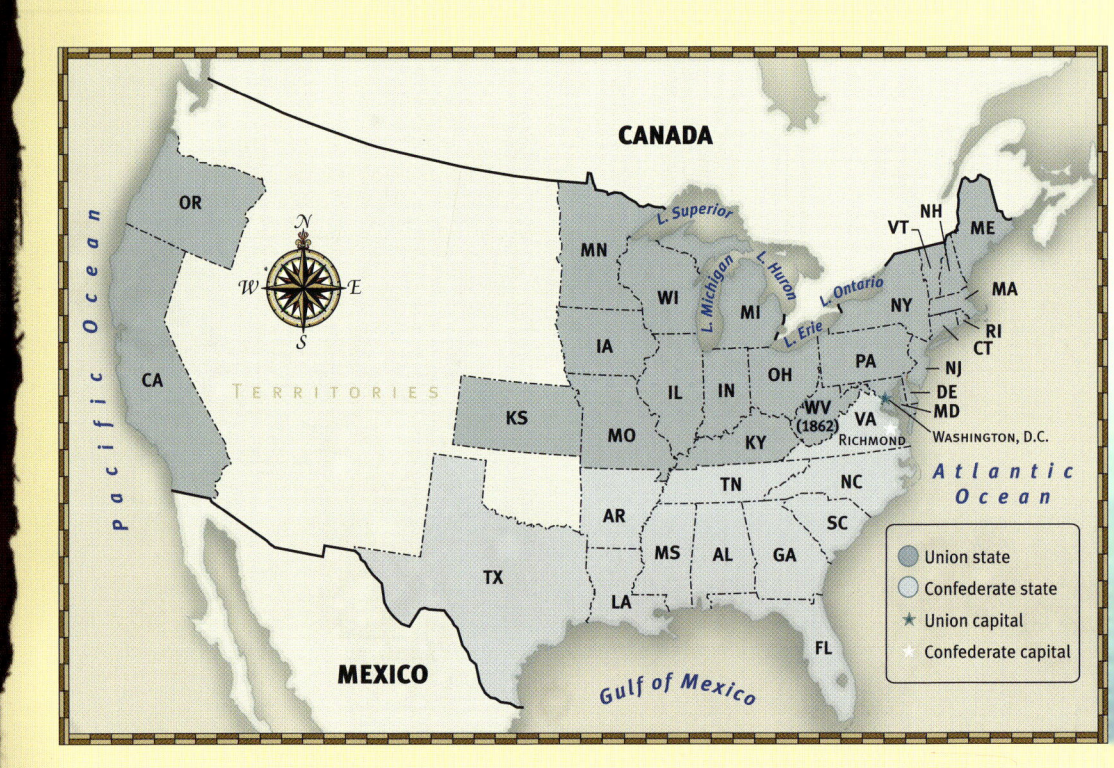

The Civil War was a long, hard war. It was fought between the North and the South. More than 600,000 Americans died during the fighting. That's more deaths than in any war before or since.

The fighting ended over one hundred years ago.

The soldiers who waged the war are long dead. The fields where they fought are peaceful now. Many battlefields have been turned into national parks.

So is the war ancient history? No. In fact, many people think of the Civil War as the first modern war.

New and improved weapons and materials changed the way that wars were fought. On land, guns could shoot straighter and farther. At sea, ships with iron plates for armor were stronger and safer than the older wooden ships.

Other discoveries allowed doctors to provide better treatment to their patients. New inventions moved people and information faster than ever before.

The Civil War put these new technologies to work. The war became a testing ground for much of what people had thought, learned about, and discovered in the years before.

▼ The British ship HMS *Warrior* was built in 1860. It was one of the first ships with iron sides.

▲ Revolutionary War musket

CHAPTER 1

The Tools of War

What are the tools of war? Guns. At the start of the Civil War, many soldiers had guns called muskets. These old guns had two big drawbacks.

First, the smooth surface inside the gun barrel made it hard to shoot straight because the bullet could not spin. Instead, it rattled its way out of the gun. A bullet could go in almost any direction. That meant that the gun's aim was good for only about 100 yards (91 meters).

The **rifle** solved this problem. Rifles had barrels with grooves, or long, narrow cuts, inside. The grooves gave the bullet spin. A bullet fired from a rifle could fly straight and far—up to 1,000 yards (914 meters).

THEY MADE A DIFFERENCE

In the late 1840s, Samuel Colt opened a factory in Hartford, Connecticut. He had designed a new gun. Colt used parts that were carefully measured and made to be exactly the same in each gun. This helped make high-quality guns. Colt could make them quickly, too. Shortly before the Civil War began, his factory could turn out 100 guns a day!

The second problem with the old type of gun was the amount of time it took to load between shots. Even a skilled soldier could take no more than five shots a minute.

One step in improving firing speed was to make a gun that could be loaded from the rear of the barrel, instead of the front. Loading from the back was called breech loading. Breech loading allowed soldiers to reload and fire more than twice as fast.

Another invention that helped soldiers fire more quickly was the repeating rifle. After it fired one bullet, another was automatically loaded. Soldiers could shoot seven or more bullets without stopping to reload. The new weapons changed the way wars were fought.

▲ The Gatling gun had six barrels. This allowed each barrel to cool off between shots.

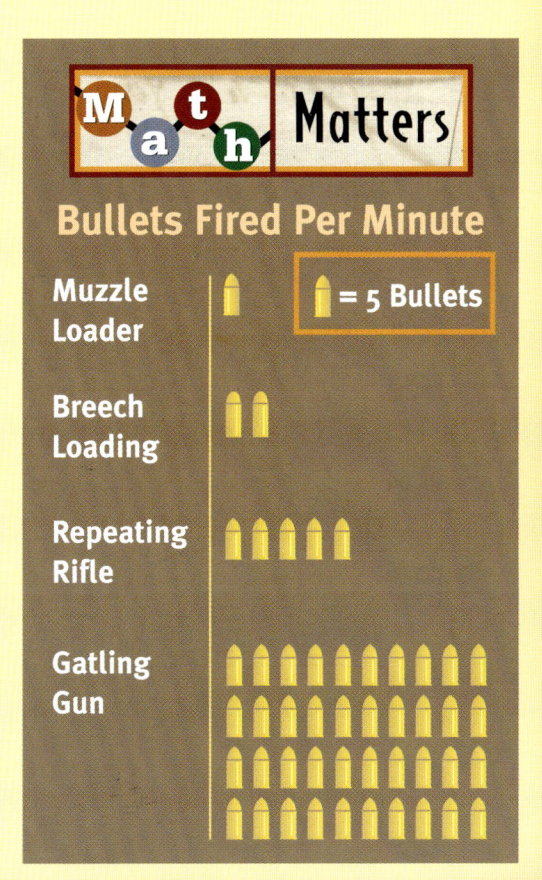

Math Matters

Bullets Fired Per Minute

Gun	Bullets
Muzzle Loader	1
Breech Loading	2
Repeating Rifle	5
Gatling Gun	40

= 5 Bullets

CHAPTER 1

The Ironclads Arrive

Early in the war, the South recovered the USS *Merrimack*. It was a wooden frigate (FRIH-guht), or warship, that belonged to the North. The ship was burned and damaged. But the South needed all the ships they could get, so they rebuilt it as an **ironclad**. They used thick iron plates to cover the **hull**, or body, of the ship for protection. When the work was done, the ship was launched as the CSS *Virginia*.

In the meantime, the North had been working on its own ironclad. Named the *Monitor*, it looked like a steel-plated raft. The ship sat low in the water, which made it hard to hit. Also, its iron plates protected it.

On March 8, 1862, the *Virginia* fought for the first time. In one afternoon, it sank two wooden ships. Two more ran aground during the battle. The wooden ships posed no threat to the ironclad.

▼ The *Monitor* was described as "a cheese box on a raft."

THE TOOLS OF WAR

▲ The *Monitor* and the *Virginia* blasted each other from close range with little effect.

The next day, the *Monitor* arrived on the scene. For three hours, it battled the *Virginia*. But neither ship was able to get the upper hand. Even direct hits did nothing more than dent or crack their thick protective plates. The battle ended in a draw.

There was one clear loser, though: wooden ships. From that day on, countries around the world worked to turn their wooden navy ships to ironclads.

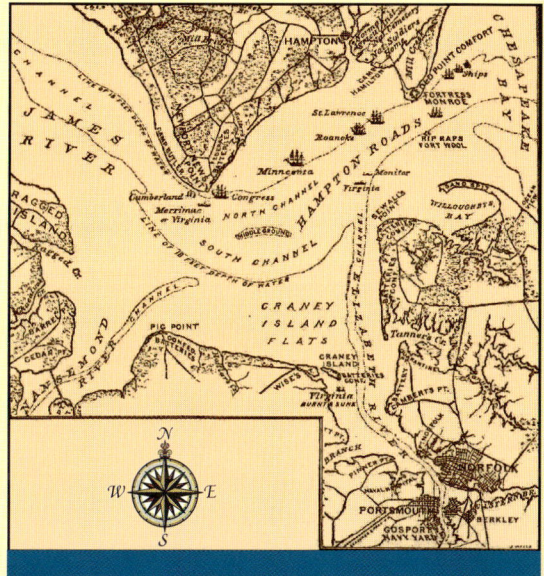

▲ This historic map shows the location of the battle between the *Virginia* and the *Monitor*.

7

CHAPTER 1

Submarine Attack

War on the water was changing in other ways, too. The South protected its ports with naval **mines**. These were designed to explode when a ship hit them. Mines sank almost thirty of the North's ships during the war.

The South also built submarines. One, the *Hunley*, was about forty feet (12.2 meters) long. Nine men on its small crew moved it through the water by turning a long hand crank attached to the propeller. The captain steered.

The *Hunley* Surfaces

On May 3, 1995, the wreck of the *Hunley* was found. It lay in thirty feet (9.1 meters) of water off the coast of South Carolina. The question was, could it be raised safely? Engineers came up with a plan in which divers would slip straps under the sub's wreckage. The straps would be attached to a frame. This could then be used to raise the wreck. It worked! In August of 2000, the *Hunley* surfaced for the first time since its historic mission.

▲ This painting of the *Hunley* was based on sketches made of the craft before it sank.

Tests of the *Hunley* showed just how dangerous it was—to its crew! It sank in two test runs. Thirteen men lost their lives. But the South chose to try the boat in action anyway.

The *Hunley*'s first mission was on February 17, 1864. That night, it sneaked up to one of the North's ships anchored off the coast of South Carolina. The sub planted a mine on the ship and began to back away. The mine exploded and ripped a hole in the ship's hull. It quickly sank. Unfortunately, so did the *Hunley*. The mission was a success because, for the first time in history, a submarine had sunk a ship.

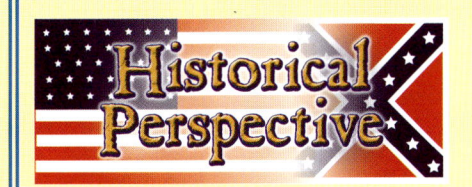

Historical Perspective

▼ The Civil War submarines had room for only one man to stand. The rest of the crew had to sit and crank the propeller.

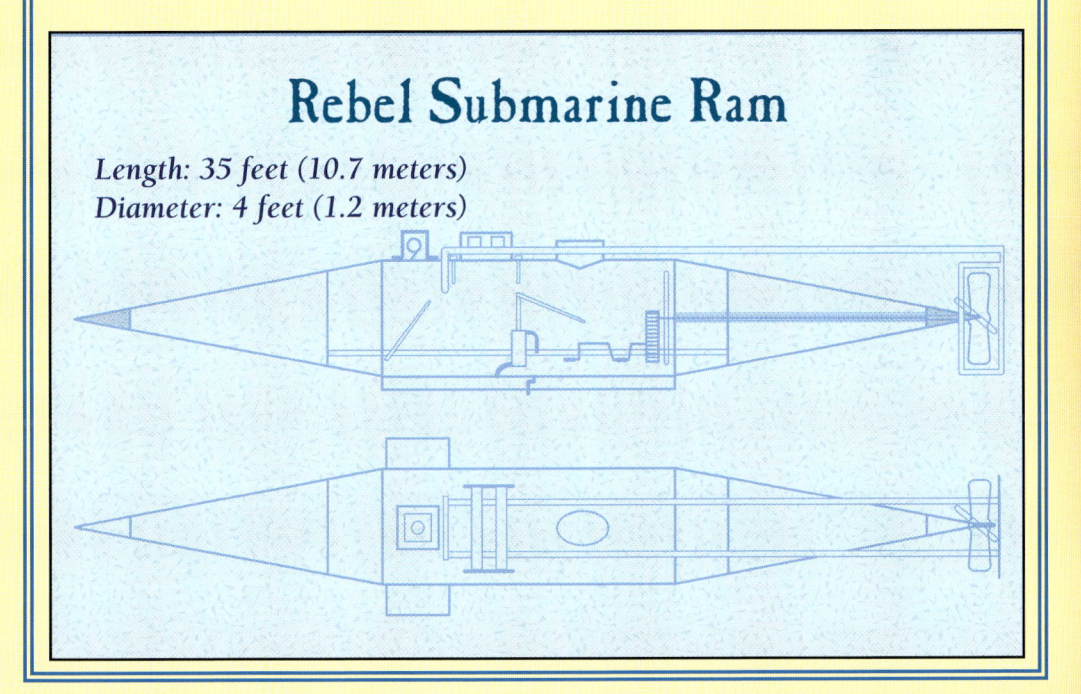

Rebel Submarine Ram

Length: 35 feet (10.7 meters)
Diameter: 4 feet (1.2 meters)

CHAPTER 1

Balloon Spies

Some people thought balloons could be useful in the war.

The balloons were sewn out of silk or another cloth. Then the cloth was covered with varnish, which made it airtight.

One balloon used by the South was sewn from silk normally used for dresses. This "balloon of many colors" came to be known as the Silk Dress Balloon.

The South only used hot air balloons. The air inside these balloons had to be heated to make them rise.

The North used gas-filled balloons. The gas inside these balloons did not need to be heated.

▼ The balloons used for watching enemy troops had to be tied to the ground.

THE TOOLS OF WAR

Observers rode in a basket attached to the bottom of a balloon. From the air, they reported what they saw to people on the ground.

The North formed the Balloon Corps (KOR). The members of the corps weren't part of the army, but they helped the army by using their bird's-eye views to report on troop movements. They often came under fire from the enemy.

This was a whole new way of spying, but many of the army officers were not sure how to use it. About halfway through the war, the corps was disbanded.

Eyewitness Account

Thaddeus Lowe was a member of the North's army. He tells how he used his balloon to spy on some enemy soldiers one night. They were trying to flee one of their forts:

"It was through the midnight observations with one of my war balloons that I was [able] to discover that the [fort was] being evacuated.... The entire great fortress was ablaze with bonfires, and the greatest activity [was going on], which was not visible except from the balloon."

▼ Thaddeus Lowe flew several balloon missions during the war.

✓ Point

Make Connections
Have you seen a hot air balloon in another photograph, a news program, or a movie? If so, who was riding in the basket? Why? Would you like to ride in a hot air balloon someday? Why or why not?

CHAPTER 2

Medical Care in the War

Civil War doctors had a tough job. They had to take care of large numbers of men with serious wounds. Most of the doctors had never seen these kinds of war wounds before. They had to learn how to treat them as they worked.

Many wounds were so bad that doctors could not cure them. As a result, there were many **amputations** (am-pyoo-TAY-shuhnz) during the war. Many soldiers lost arms or legs. Doctors learned how to amputate quickly. A good doctor could remove a limb in ten minutes.

Perhaps the most important thing doctors learned was ligation (lie-GAY-shuhn). This was a way to sew shut arteries, or main blood vessels, that had been cut in surgery.

▼ This camp portrait shows Union Surgeon Jonathan Letterman and his staff. Letterman is given credit for the Civil War field hospital system.

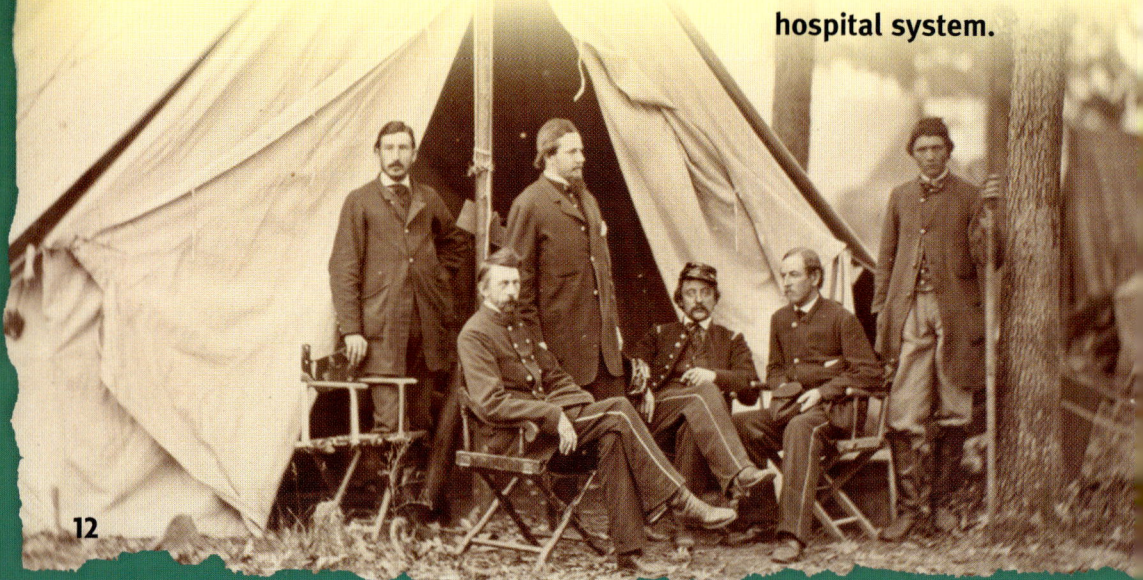

Doctors knew how to use **anesthesia** (a-nuhs-TEE-zhuh) by the time of the Civil War. Anesthesia eased the pain a patient experienced during an operation.

Patients were anesthetized using special gases. They usually breathed in the gas through a piece of cloth. Then their senses became dull.

It's a FACT

Amputation was the most common surgery during the Civil War. In the Union army alone, 30,000 men lost limbs. Doctors needed to have a saw in their medical kits to do this job. This led to a gruesome nickname for the doctors: "sawbones."

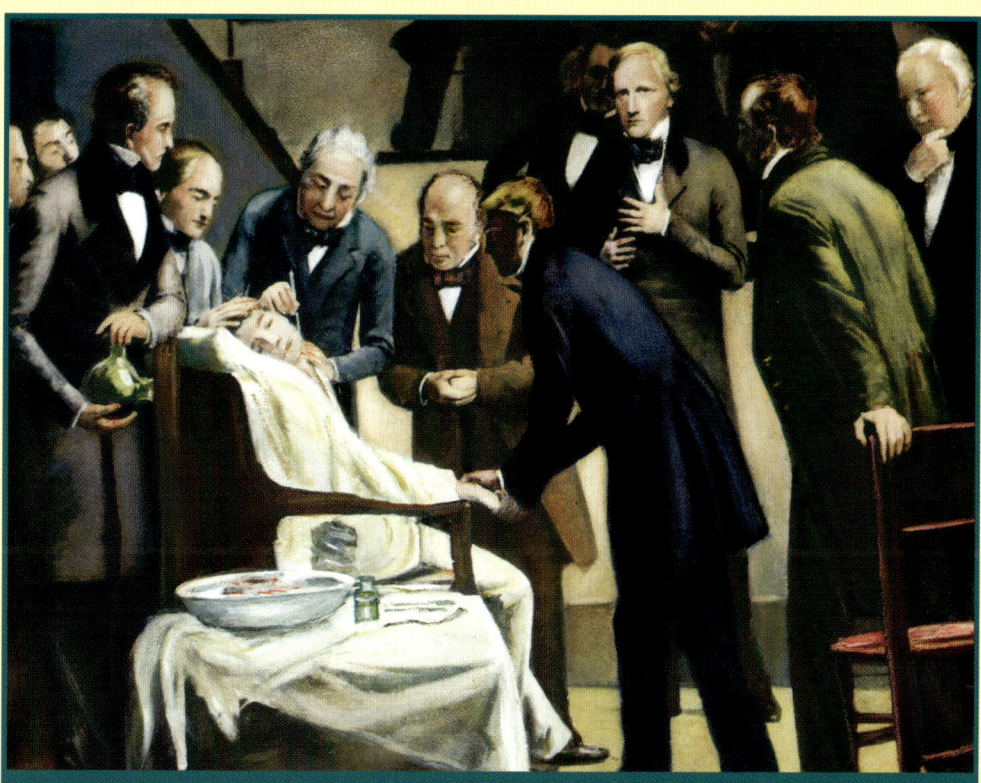

▲ This doctor is giving his patient anesthesia before surgery.

CHAPTER 2

It's a FACT

Gangrene developed after one out of every five operations.

THEY MADE A DIFFERENCE

Two years after the war ended, Joseph Lister discovered how to sterilize wounds, or make them perfectly clean. That knowledge would have saved tens of thousands of lives during the war.

Infection and Amputation

Civil War doctors made advances in the use of anesthesia, but they didn't know about germs and how they cause infections. Doctors didn't keep their hands, clothes, or instruments clean. They cleaned their instruments with water.

Because of this, soldiers often made it through surgery, but then died from infection. Some got blood poisoning. Others got gangrene (gang-GREEN), which ate away at their wounds.

When a soldier grew sick after surgery, doctors said he had a "surgical fever." They didn't know that their unclean practices had caused it.

For many soldiers, surgery meant amputation. The government wanted to help those soldiers. They promised to give every man who lost a limb his own **prosthesis** (prahs-TEE-sihs), or artificial limb, to replace it.

MEDICAL CARE IN THE WAR

Tens of thousands of men needed new limbs. To meet the need, many businesses were started to design and sell prostheses. People came up with ways to make the prostheses for war **veterans** (VEH-tuh-ruhnz), people who had been in the armed forces, better. One big advance was the use of rubber, which made the limbs more flexible and easier to control.

▲ This man has two artificial legs.

It's a FACT

People in the South had a hard time getting medicines during the war. Shipping routes were often blocked so medicines couldn't reach the South. A surgeon named Francis Porcher prepared a special report. He told doctors how to use leaves, stems, and the roots of plants and trees to replace the missing medicines. Porcher wrote about plants that could make a patient sleepy, ease pain, or stop the flow of blood.

CHAPTER 2

Disease and Sanitation

The camps were dirty and crowded. Soldiers suffered through heat, cold, rain, and snow. They were underfed. Mosquitoes and other bugs attacked them. All this increased the odds that the men would become ill. Sometimes so many men were sick that a general couldn't take his army into battle.

Dysentery (DIH-suhn-tair-ee), typhoid (TIE-foid), and malaria (muh-LAIR-ee-uh) killed many men. For every soldier that died of battle wounds, two died of disease.

Eyewitness Account

A doctor from the South wrote about how disease struck the army:
"There was an epidemic of measles in the army [and] every soldier who had not been 10 miles from his home before he enlisted was seized with it. I've had boys of 16 [and] fathers of 60 years lying side by side on straw beds placed on the floor, all suffering from measles or some of its complications."

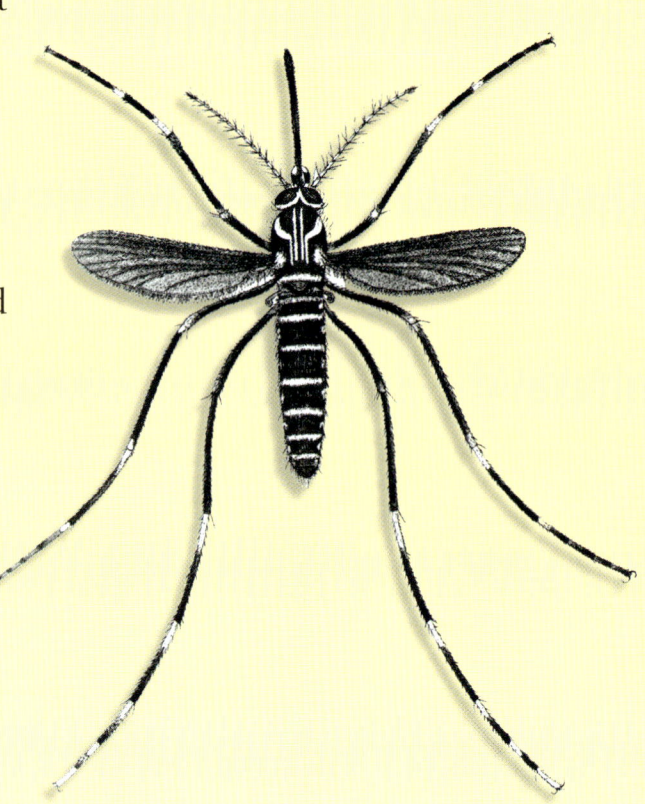

▲ Mosquitoes brought deadly malaria to the soldiers.

MEDICAL CARE IN THE WAR

It soon became clear that the camps were a big health problem. In the North, the Sanitary Commission was formed to improve soldiers' health. One of its jobs was to come up with health guidelines for the army. But its work was also hands-on. Surgeons and nurses tended to the sick. Volunteers taught soldiers how to keep camps clean. Away from the front lines, they also collected food and medicine for the soldiers. Some held fund-raisers to buy supplies.

It's a FACT

Volunteers throughout the North made more than 250,000 quilts and comforters for army camps and hospitals.

Although nursing had been a male occupation before the war, hundreds of women volunteered to become nurses during the war.

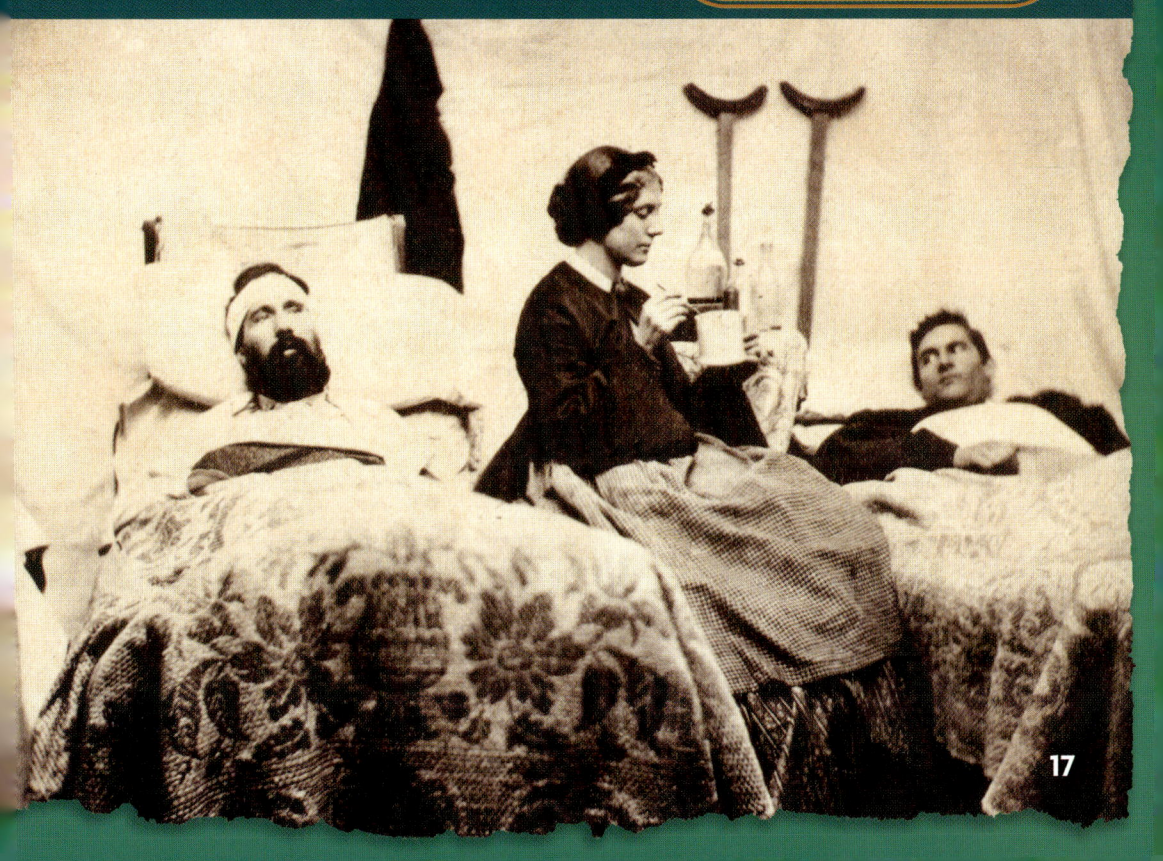

CHAPTER 2

Hospital Care

The two sides had not realized how long and hard the war would be. They were surprised by the number of sick and wounded they had to care for.

To meet the demand, they had to change how they cared for people. Older hospitals needed more staff to care for the soldiers. New hospitals had to be built.

The medical systems in both armies grew better as the war wore on. Different kinds of hospitals met different needs.

▼ These doctors performed surgery on the wounded in field hospitals near the battlefield.

MEDICAL CARE IN THE WAR

▲ The largest Civil War hospital even had its own bakery.

▲ In Civil War times, women's skirts had large hoops in them to make them full. Female nurses had to take the hoops out so they could move in the narrow aisles between the beds.

Wounded men were first treated near the battlefield. Doctors gave emergency care in field hospitals. A field hospital could be placed in a church, a house, or a school. Most were set up in tents. Doctors preferred to use tents because they offered good air circulation. Field hospitals were set back from the front lines. Most surgeries took place there.

General hospitals gave long-term care to soldiers. Most were large and far away from the fighting. The biggest was in Virginia. It had several thousand beds. A small farm nearby grew food for the soldiers.

✔ Point

Talk About It
Pretend you're a soldier in the Civil War. Tell a partner some things you might experience if you become sick or injured.

CHAPTER 2

Medics and Nurses

Early in the war, the two armies didn't have a good way to get the wounded off the battlefield. The men who carried stretchers and drove ambulances were not trained. In the thick of battle, some ran away. The ambulances were often used for other jobs.

The two sides came up with the same way to fix this problem. The North started the Ambulance Corps. The South's version was called the Infirmary Corps. These were special groups of trained medics, people who could give medical help on the battlefield. Officers were in charge of the medics and supplies, including the ambulances.

▼ Medics in the Ambulance Corps worked bravely to carry wounded soldiers off the field to safety.

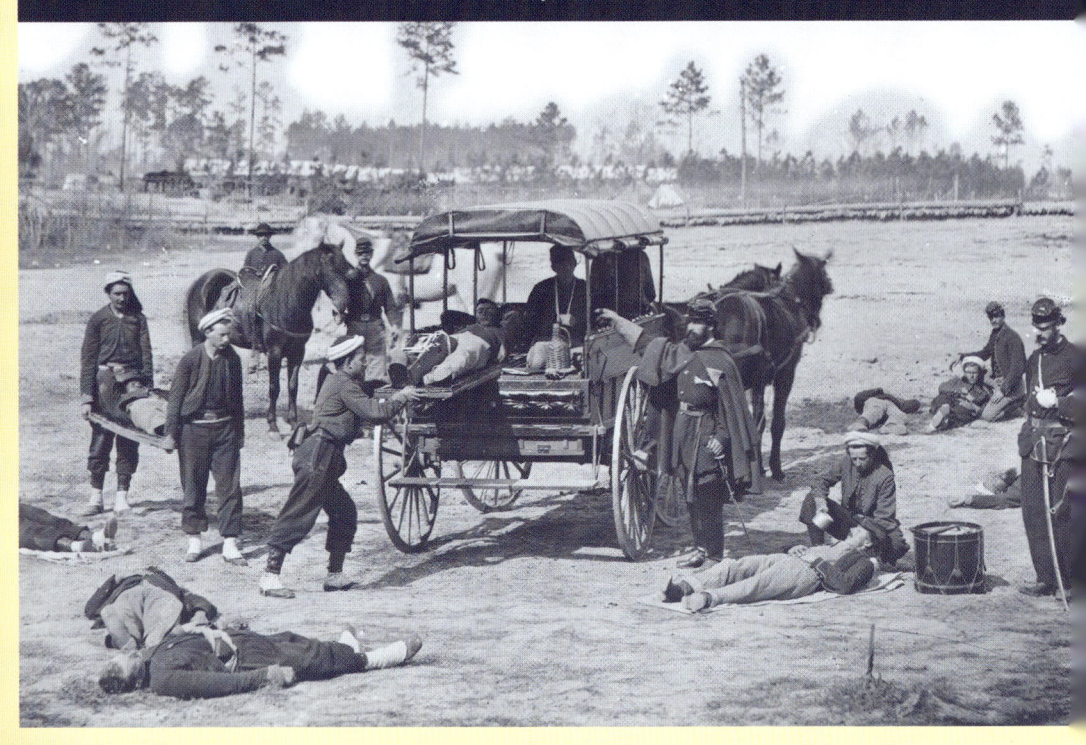

MEDICAL CARE IN THE WAR

Soldiers' care changed, too. At first, they were cared for by doctors and other soldiers. Women who wanted to help were not welcome. Many people thought women had no place in hospitals.

But there were not enough men to take care of the wounded. A few months after the war began, a woman named Dorothea Dix agreed to find and place female nurses for the North's army. Soon, women went to work.

African Americans also had to fight to help treat the wounded. Some worked as nurses. At least eight African American men served as doctors in the North's army.

THEY MADE A DIFFERENCE

Susie King Taylor was born into slavery in Georgia. She escaped in 1862. During the Civil War, she served as a nurse for Northern soldiers in South Carolina. She also taught reading and writing to many of the soldiers. Years later, she wrote a book about her experiences, called *A Black Woman's Civil War Memoirs*.

CHAPTER 3

The Spread of Information

Dot dot dash. Dash dot dot dash. These dots and dashes were part of a code used to send messages by **telegraph** (TEH-lih-graf). The messages were sent through wires strung along poles across the country. At the time of the Civil War, the telegraph was the modern way to send a message.

When the war started, there were 50,000 miles (80,467.2 kilometers) of telegraph wire across the nation. That number soon grew. Wire followed the North's troops as they fought in the South.

▼ **Union troops strung 15,000 miles (24,140.2 kilometers) of telegraph wire during the war.**

The telegraph changed the way that armies communicated. Generals could now get their news in a flash. They could "talk" with troops hundreds of miles away.

There was even a telegraph office in the War Department in Washington, D.C. Messages came in from all over the country. President Abraham Lincoln often stopped by to hear the latest war news.

Both sides also used the telegraph for spying. Listeners tapped into the other side's lines to learn about troop movements and battle plans. Special codes had to be used to keep this news safe from enemy ears.

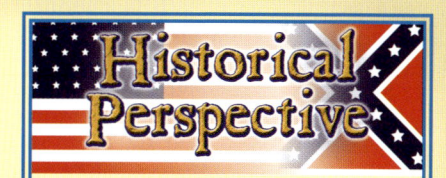

Historical Perspective

Today it's easy to get news to someone far away. All you have to do is dial a phone number or type an e-mail. But sending messages by telegraph was not so easy. Trained operators used telegraph keys to tap out combinations of long and short tones or clicks. Each combination stood for a different letter. The operator on the other end would have to decode the message and then deliver it to the person for whom it was meant.

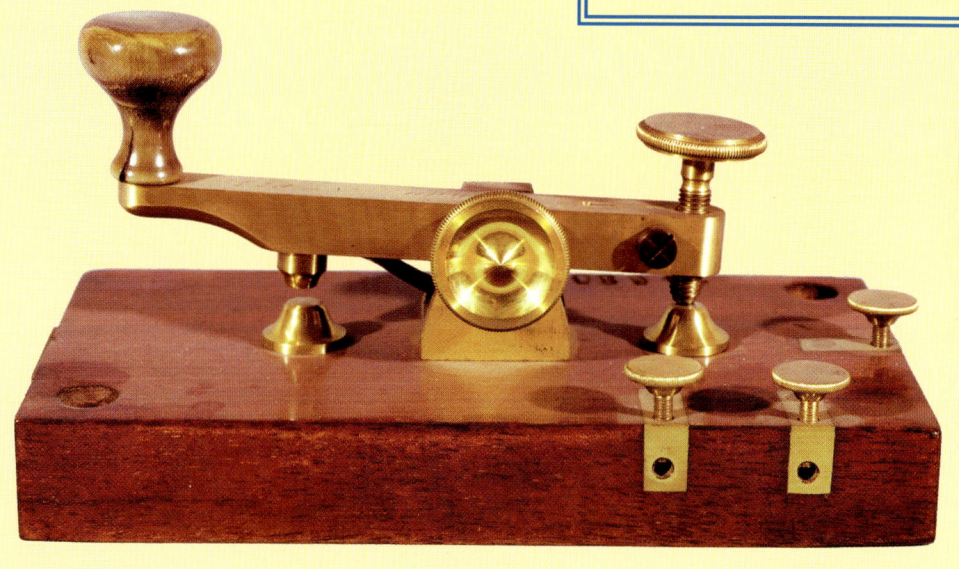

▲ Telegraph operators tapped out messages over the wires.

CHAPTER 3

Railroads

It wasn't just news that moved fast. Troops and goods did too, thanks to trains. Soldiers no longer had to rely solely on their feet or their horses. Instead, they could let the railroad do the work. Trains quickly and easily moved huge numbers of men and supplies great distances.

Both sides soon saw how important railroad lines were. Bull Run, the first big battle of the war, was fought for a railroad **junction**, where two lines met, in Virginia. Railroads remained a target all through the war.

▼ The railroad moved troops and supplies much faster than earlier methods.

THE SPREAD OF INFORMATION

As the North fought deeper into the South, it became harder to ship supplies to the troops. The railroad solved the problem.

Trains were a huge help to General William T. Sherman during his fight to take Atlanta. Day after day, enough supplies for 100,000 men and 35,000 animals arrived by trains. They came from a base far away. Sherman later wrote that bringing in supplies the old-fashioned way "would have required 36,800 wagons . . . allowing each wagon to have hauled two tons twenty miles each day." In other words, it could not have been done without the railroad.

It's a FACT

When an army captured a railroad line, they did not always use it. Sometimes they destroyed it. Sherman did this to many railroads he captured during his march across the South. His troops ripped up the tracks. Then they built fires to heat the rails until they were soft and could be bent. The rails were then twisted so they could not be reused. These tangles of metal came to be known as "Sherman's neckties."

▲ The North's strategy for weakening the South included destroying captured railroad lines.

Newspaper and the War

Reporters now followed the troops. They sent back reports of what they saw. People at home read the newspapers for the latest war news.

Reports were sent back by telegraph to the newspapers. The papers could get news of a battle into print the day after it ended.

Some people feared that news reports might give key information to the enemy. Government **censors** (SEHN-suhrz) changed some stories. They kept others from being published.

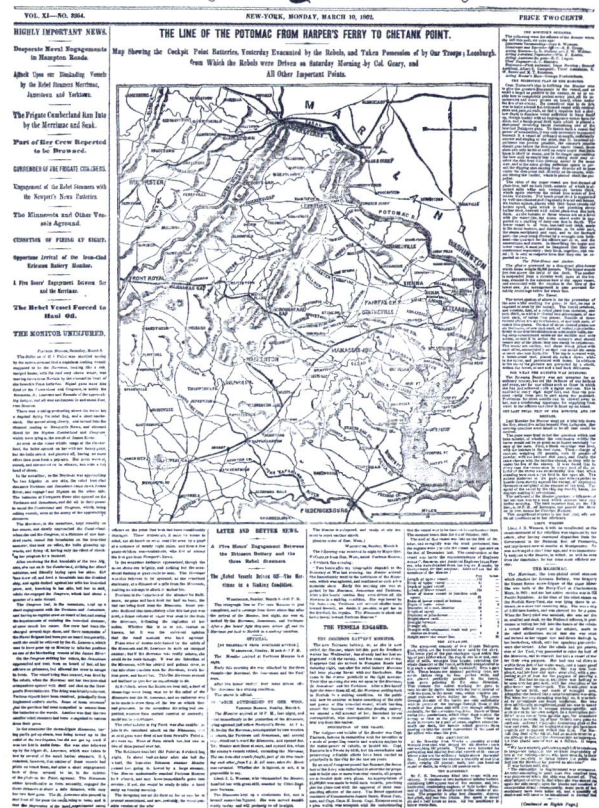

▲ People in the North and the South read newspapers to keep up with the events of the war.

CAREERS

War correspondents report from war zones around the world. Today they can file their stories using cell phones or computers. But one thing hasn't changed since the Civil War: It's very dangerous work. Some reporters travel with troops. This means that when the fighting starts, the lives of the correspondents are at risk, too.

Math Matters

At the start of the war, the North had over 20,000 miles (32,187 kilometers) of railroad track. The South had only 9,000 miles (14,484 kilometers). This gave the North a huge advantage in moving troops and supplies.

THE SPREAD OF INFORMATION

News could have a big effect on what people thought. For example, newspapers on each side accused the other of mistreating POWs (prisoners of war). Some of the stories spread rumors rather than facts. Reports told of captives forced to eat rotten food. Others said that POWs had wounds that were never treated. Some of the reports were illustrated. The drawings showed the horrors of prison life. The public was outraged.

Eyewitness Account

A correspondent for the *Philadelphia Age* wrote this description of the fighting during the Battle of Gettysburg:

"The fight swayed back and forth. One moment the enemy would be at the railings of the cemetery; then a rush from the Federal side [the North] would drive them down into the valley. Then, with one of their horrid screeches, [the enemy] would fiercely run up the hill again into the cemetery, and have a fierce battle among the tombstones. It was the hardest fight of the day, and hundreds were slain there."

▶ At the time of the Civil War, there was no way to print photographs. Instead, newspapers used drawings to illustrate their stories.

27

Photography

Photography was still new when the war started, but photographers made the most of their chance to document the war. Thousands of soldiers sat for portraits. Some of these were shot in studios in cities and towns. Others were made by photographers who moved from camp to camp.

One type of portrait was the *carte de visité* (KAHRT duh vee-zee-TAY). It could be copied easily. Soldiers could give prints to their friends and families. Some people even collected *cartes de visité* of the famous—much like collecting baseball cards.

▲ carte de visité

▲ This photograph shows the ruins of Charleston after it was captured by the North.

THE SPREAD OF INFORMATION

Some photographers took battlefield photos. They could not take action shots. Their cameras were too slow for that. Instead, they took pictures after the battles ended. Some showed soldiers at their moment of triumph. Others showed the horrors of the dead and wounded.

One man, Matthew Brady, had a crew of over 100 people who worked to photograph the war. The newspapers at the time were not able to print the photographs. So Brady held showings where people could view them. *The New York Times* wrote that the photos showed "the terrible reality . . . of war."

Historical Perspective

In its early days, photography was not simple. Pictures were not captured on film. Instead, photographers used big glass plates. They had to coat the plates with chemicals to capture images. Also, cameras were big and bulky. Photographers had to use carts to move their supplies around.

▲ The carts that photographers used to move their supplies were nicknamed "whatsit wagons" by the soldiers.

Conclusion

The Civil War was the cause behind many new inventions. These inventions changed the way wars were fought. Improved guns could shoot farther and were more accurate. Ships and submarines changed war at sea. Railroads moved troops and supplies farther and faster. The telegraph made spreading news quicker. Photography allowed people to see what war was really like.

To help the wounded, doctors found better ways of treating their patients. Nursing saved many lives. These inventions were created in war time, but they also became important in remaking people's lives. So many things we take for granted were invented to fight the Civil War. The inventions of war made the future peace time better.

▼ After the Civil War, the number of patents granted greatly increased.

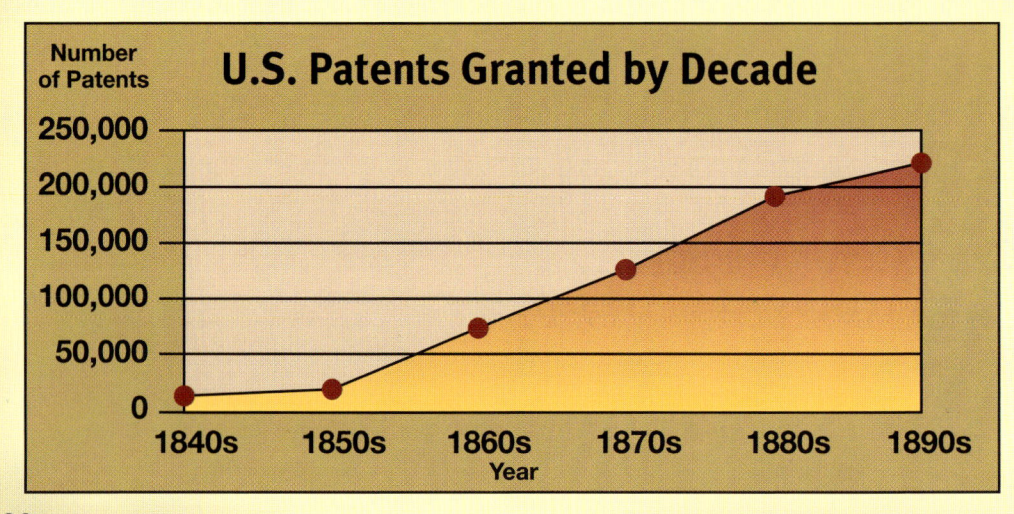

U.S. Patents Granted by Decade

Glossary

amputation (am-pyoo-TAY-shuhn) cutting off part or all of an arm or leg (page 12)

anesthesia (a-nuhs-TEE-zhuh) the loss of all feeling, especially pain (page 13)

censor (SEHN-suhr) a person who examines personal mail or other material and removes information considered secret (page 26)

hull (HUHL) the main body of a ship (page 6)

ironclad (EYE-uhrn-klad) a ship covered with metal plates for armor (page 6)

junction (JUHNGK-shuhn) a place where two or more roads or railroads meet (page 24)

mine (MINE) an explosive device that is set off by something else touching it (page 8)

prosthesis (prahs-TEE-sihs) a replacement for a missing body part (page 14)

rifle (RY-fuhl) a gun with spiral grooves cut into the barrel to improve its accuracy and range (page 4)

telegraph (TEH-lih-graf) an electrical system for communicating messages using codes (page 22)

veteran (VEH-tuh-ruhn) a person who has served in the armed forces (page 15)

Index

Ambulance Corps, 20
amputation, 12, 14
anesthesia, 13, 30
balloon, 10–11
censor, 26
disease, 16
hospital, 18–19, 21
hull, 6, 9
infection, 14
ironclad, 6–7
junction, 24
Lincoln, Abraham, 23
medical care, 12–21
mine, 8–9

newspaper, 26–27, 29
nurse, 17, 21
photography, 28–30
prosthesis, 14–15, 30
railroad, 24–25, 30
rifle, 4–5
sanitation, 16–17
Sanitation Commission, 17
Sherman, William, 25
spying, 11, 23
submarine, 8–9, 30
telegraph, 22–23, 26, 30
veteran, 15